Made in the USA
Middletown, DE
29 August 2023

37552872R00057